Foster Care and Me

An autobiographical account of the challenges faced and
overcome on a journey
from Foster Care to Care Leaver
to becoming an influential Social Entrepreneur

Change Is Possible!

To Matthew,
A pleasure
to have met
you. Keep
wanting a
difference,
because you can!
All the Best
Judith APRIL 2023

Written by

Judith A.M. Denton

Grosvenor House
Publishing Limited

This book is published by
Grosvenor House Publishing Ltd
Link House
140 The Broadway, Tolworth, Surrey, KT6 7HT.
www.grosvenorhousepublishing.co.uk

A CIP record for this book
is available from the British Library

ISBN 978-1-78623-642-5

Contents

Acknowledgements   v

Introduction   vii

Foster Care

Chapter 1 – Foster Care   3

Chapter 2 – Foster Care, Secondary School, College
and the Law   7

Chapter 3 – Foster Care, University and Law School   15

Care Leaver

Chapter 4 – Care Leaver and Leaving Home   21

Chapter 5 – Care Leaver, My Mental Health and
Therapy   25

Chapter 6 – Care Leaver and My Career   31

Chapter 7 – Care Leaver and Becoming a
Social Entrepreneur   35

Messages

To Children and Young People in Care
and Care Leavers   49

To Foster Carers   55

To Schools and Social Workers   63

CONTENTS

To our Prime Minister, UK Parliament,
Secretary of State for Education Parliamentary
Under Secretary of State for Children and
Families Ofsted Chief Inspector and
the Children's Commissioner for England   71

This is not 'The End'

Epilogue   81

Acknowledgements

To my Foster Parents, Mr and Mrs Laws. Thank you for welcoming me into your home and into your hearts. We had our ups and downs, but you did not give up on me. The seeds you have planted in my life, have taken root and have begun to blossom. Mum, Erna Vermir Laws, I wish you were here to see me now. May you rest in eternal peace.

To my Brother, Nicholas Denton. I'm proud to be your little big sister. We've been through so much together and apart, but look at us now. I love you and I enjoy doing life with you.

To my Mum Gwen and Dad Owen, as an adult, I've come to learn that life happens to the best of us. I love you both.

To my Mentors and Trusted Advisors, Mr Carver Anderson, Mrs Pauline Mckenzie and Mr Herman Allen. You all came into my life at exactly the right time. Thank you for being there, when I couldn't fathom my way forward. Your consistent insight, prayers and straight talking, encouraged, challenged and empowered me to learn how to crawl, walk, run, fly and not give up. It is said *Without good direction, people loose their way, the more wise counsel you follow, the better your chances.* I am honoured to have you all in my life, for life.

To my fabulous, fun, loving, lively, core Support Network of Friends, I don't want to start naming names, just in case I forget anyone, so I'm going to say YOU KNOW WHO YOU ARE! Thank you for sticking with me through the 'real real' and celebrating with me on the otherside. I love you all!

To my Mentees, you have helped to inspire me to write this book. Walking with you through your Foster Care journey, has provided me with first-hand insight into how the United Kingdom Care System has changed and still needs to change, in order to continue to make a lasting difference in the lives of others like us. Keep your heads up, you're going to make it, I am proud of you!

And last, but by no means least, to God, my Heavenly Father, to you I sing the song You gave me, *For Your Glory, For Your Glory, Created for Your Glory, Positioned for Purpose, Designed for Destiny, For Your Glory, For Your Glory, Created for Your Glory, Establish oh Awesome One, the Work You've done in me.*

Introduction

Research states,

Children in Care are likely to have complex and challenging needs and must overcome extra challenges to achieve their potential.

They are also sometimes regarded as low achievers with low life chances on route to being a financial burden to the state, being a part of their own dysfunctional family, being homeless, having a lower take up of education, employment and training, poor mental and physical health outcomes in adulthood, have higher reoffending rates and placed at Her Majesty's Pleasure.[1]

With that in mind, please let me introduce myself.

My name is Judith A.M. Denton and I was placed in Foster Care at the age of nine.

Growing up through the system, I experienced exclusions from school and college, a run-in with the law, and then as a Care Leaver, I experienced a period of poor mental health, so you could say that I was near enough a statistic found within the above research.

---

[1] Research gained from:
National Audit Office report 'Children In Care' – 25 November 2014 | Ofsted Pupil Premium Report – 2013

BUT hold on, my story doesn't end there...

In order to recover, mentally, emotionally and physically, with the advice and guidance of my Mentor, Mr Carver Anderson, I embarked on a journey through therapy, that caused me to find the courage to break the silence, take off the mask I had worn from the age of nine into my late twenties and come face to face with the pain I had internalised by feeling rejected, abandoned and unloved, as a result of being placed in the System.

This process was by no means a quick process, but through it I reconciled with and accepted my past, and was now curious about who I had become and what I could achieve, and so I was ready for a fresh start on this journey called 'Life'.

Without giving too much away at this stage, I can say that through the pages of this book, I provide an in-depth account of each stage of my journey and the challenges faced, from being in Foster Care to becoming a Care Leaver and now a Social Entrepreneur, to bring hope to Children and Young People in Care and Care Leavers, to see that they don't have to fall into the negative statistics of research bodies, but rather hear real and tangible evidence to see and believe that Change Is Possible for them too, and not to give up!

I've also written this book for Foster Carers, Social Workers, Supervising Social Workers, Designated Teachers, School Staff, Virtual Schools, our Prime Minister, Secretary of State for Education, and (our Children's Minister) also known as the Parliamentary Under Secretary of State for Children and Families, Ofsted and our Children's Commissioner, to help provide insight into how together, we can change the trajectory and improve the outcomes and life chances of our Children and Young People in Care and Care Leavers.

I've also written this book for those who have not been in Care, but have experienced or are experiencing the challenges this life can bring. May my story ignite in you hope to believe that you too can move forward to live and thrive.

Foster Care

Children and Young People of all ages and from all backgrounds come into Care when they are unable to live with their birth parents for a period of time. Foster Care can give families a chance to sort out their problems by providing these children with a home and supportive family for as long as they need. When the decision is made to take a child into Care, the Local Authority becomes responsible for his or her welfare.

The Fostering Network
www.thefosteringnetwork.org.uk

Chapter 1 – Foster Care

It's early in the morning, I can't remember what day it is and I don't know what time it is, but I remember my mum getting me and my brother ready for something, and I'm not sure what this 'something' is. I'm washed, creamed and clothed and I watch a suitcase being packed.

I hear a knock at the front door, it's our family friend Winston. He smiles and says *"Are you ready?"* I don't know what he's talking about and I can't remember where my brother is at this point. I remember my mum hugging me and saying *"I'll see you soon"* and then I'm led to Winston's taxi.

It's quiet in the car. I'm unsure of where I'm going. *Did anyone tell me?* I don't remember, but it's quiet in the car. About ten minutes later, Winston parks the car outside a house. He opens the car door to where I'm sitting and helps me out. He opens a light green gate to a concrete path that leads to a very large looking house and I see the number 140. He has in his hand, the suitcase that I saw my mum pack and I realise it's mine. He rings the door bell, which has a piercing sound. I'm calm, but at the same time wondering, *Who's going to open the door and why am I here?"* Winston holds my hand, looks at me and says *"You're going to be OK."*

It's not long, before the door is opened by a man who I recognise, but can't remember his name. Winston and this man greet each other and my suitcase is handed over. I'm also greeted and welcomed in, as Winston says, "Goodbye".

I was nine years old, approaching my tenth birthday.

I stand in the hallway, unsure of what to do. The man asks me if I am OK and I reply *"Yes"*. I think I remember being told that my room wasn't ready and that I was to go upstairs to my Godmother. *Godmother?! who's that?* I thought. I think the man, realised that I'd never been to this house before and led me up two flights of stairs. As he opens the door to what I now know is a bedroom, I hear *"Hello Judith are you all right?"*

I recognise the voice and I recognise the face. It's Mrs Laws the lady from church. I'm slightly at ease, when I see her and quickly have an "ah hah" moment as I remember who the man is, it's her husband, Mr Laws, also from church.

Godmother!? Now I remember hearing people say that she is my Godmother, but I'd never spent any time with her and so didn't really know her. I remember that she used to visit our home from time to time, but that was it. Was Mr Laws my Godfather too? Yes.

As she looked at me, I remember she smiled and said, *"It's too early for you to go to school, come and lay down and I'll get you up and take you. When you come home from school, your room will be ready"*. I hesitantly, took my shoes off, climbed up on the bed, that seemed to be unusually high, and lay there in silence. Mrs Laws must have dozed off as I could hear her breathing. I lay there thinking, *What am I doing here? Where's my mum and where's my brother?* I lay there for what seemed to be hours, until Mrs Laws woke up and took me downstairs for breakfast and then took me to school, Cutlers Brook Junior School.

As I'm writing this, I can't remember how long it was before I realised that this could potentially be my new home. I say 'potentially' because, there was a series of events which led to this being my reality.

After a few months, my mum returned. *Yes!* I thought, *Now I can go home.* Don't get me wrong, I liked being with Mr and Mrs Laws, but I missed my mum and especially my older brother. I came to find out that he was also living with his Godparents and we'd get to see each other at church on Sundays or at the church Youth Club on Wednesday evenings, and his name is Nicholas (Nick or Nicky for short) and he was ten years old approaching his eleventh birthday at the time.

With Mum returning, I couldn't understand why we didn't all go back to our house at 16 Warminster Road in Bristol. She came and stayed with me for a bit at Mr and Mrs Laws' house, and I assume she went to stay with my brother, but we were never all in the same place at the same time. On a visit to stay with me, I remember, after having a bath, my mum sat with me on my bed and told me she was going to live in America and was not coming back. I looked at her in silence. How did she expect this nine-year-old kid to respond? I climbed into bed and went to sleep, in silence.

I don't know how, but I found out that Mum had come back to England to finalise her divorce with Dad and make arrangements as to who was going to take care of me and my brother.

The original plan was for both of us to live with our Auntie in London, (my mum's sister), but that plan didn't materialise.

It was then decided that my brother and I would be placed in Foster Care for the short term, as my mum had plans for us to live with her in America, once she had settled down.

The day came for Mum to leave the UK. I don't remember how, but my brother and I accompanied her to Bristol Bus and Coach Station. As she boarded the train, I watched as tears streamed down her face and she said, "Goodbye," and that she was sorry. My brother broke down and I had to hold him. He was crying, sobbing, pleading with our Mum not to go. I was silent. No tears. I had to be strong for my brother as I held him. She got off the coach, and I thought, *She's changed her mind, she's staying.* She ran to us, hugged and kissed us, tears still streaming down her face, and then got back on the coach. I screamed inside, but there was no sound. She'd gone.

Now I knew for sure, that living with Mr and Mrs Laws was indeed my new home, my new reality, my Foster Carers.

Chapter 2 – Foster Care, Secondary School, College and the Law

I'm now eleven years old and attending a new school, Fairfield Grammar School, which is five minutes' walk from my new home. I had to sit, and pass, an English test to be able to get in. I remember, I was asked to write a short story, which seemed to get me the pass mark needed.

I now have a Social Worker, called Jeanne Gilraine. She was really nice to me and my brother, always making time for us, taking us out on activities to make sure we saw each other on a regular basis.

On one occasion, I remember her asking us if we wanted to go and live with either our Mum or our Dad. Together, my brother and I decided we wanted to stay in Bristol. I made this decision as I felt I was settled and didn't know what life would be like with either parent and at this stage, I really didn't want to know. I think my brother had the same thought process, as I remember Jeanne letting us know that she felt we were very mature for our age, because of the reasons why we wanted to stay in Bristol.

Later on in life, I came to understand that both our parents were making plans for us to live with them, however, Mum's hope of us living with her did not materialise, as life in the USA did not start off as well as she had hoped, and my Dad's plan to move us to Germany also fell through. Needless to say, we were already of the view that Bristol was to be our home, which is what we knew and believed was where we belonged.

School was fun. I made new friends and there were people that I knew within the community that also attended Fairfield. One of my younger cousins also came to the same school the year after I started.

Now, my older cousins had attended this school and it seemed as if the school staff had an expectation of what I would be like, because of the good reputation of my older cousins, but I was not to be compared to them. You see whilst I enjoyed being at school, I didn't always like being at school, there were days I didn't want to learn and I made a point of letting the class and the teacher know. There were days when I wanted the lessons to be a bit more exciting and would add that excitement into the flow of every lesson. My school reports said I was "capable", but I couldn't see it. My school reports also said I needed to "stop distracting the class and pay more attention".

In all honesty, I felt "vulnerable". I'd always gone to the same school as my brother and now he was nowhere to be seen, living in a new home and attending a new school.

During one visit to my Foster Care home, my brother let me know that I had to look after myself, because he wasn't around to look after me, and so got to teaching me how to roll my fists and fight. I'm not sure if this was because he sensed that I might be bullied or that he wanted to make sure that if I got into a fight, I'd know how to handle myself.

I don't remember how long it took, before I had my first fight at school and then one became a few and then a few more. I'd say I was defending myself, whenever I was teased or laughed at or called a name, and I'll be honest to admit that I gave as good as I got in that department. But as a result of the constant fights, being sent out of lessons along with a series of detentions, I was often sent home, excluded from school for up to five days at a time and returning to attend return to school meetings with my Foster Mum and my Social Worker and whichever Teacher was available. There I would hear that this was my last chance or I'd be expelled and moved to another school. I was never expelled and I think this was because of my Foster Mum, who at every meeting, would listen and respectfully let the Teachers know that, *"Judith will be behaving this time"*.

Now, I did try to knuckle down and get on in school when I returned, but I still felt "vulnerable", "alone", "not wanting to be there", but couldn't express how I felt. I'd laugh and joke with my friends. Sometimes I felt that I didn't "fit in", but needless to say I carried on as if I did.

A fight during lunch time, led to me being permanently excluded from school for only the lunch period. I was escorted off the school premises at lunch time and only allowed back in school after lunch. My Foster Mum had also become a dinner lady at the school and so I couldn't even get away with hanging around. I remember, when she was informed of this way forward, that she said to me that I was lucky to not have been expelled, but if I didn't stop fighting, I would end up in deeper trouble and when that day came, I was not to call her.

Whilst at school, there were two teachers, who I sensed, genuinely had time for me and believed in me. This was Ms Wanless, who taught Art and Mr Baber, who taught Biology.

I remember after another fight, I felt really fed up and angry. I hadn't started the fight and had just wanted to be left alone. I made my way to Ms Wanless' Art Room and burst into tears. She was teaching at the time, saw me and beckoned for me to sit at the back of the classroom, until I was OK.

I didn't completely understand Biology, but I liked being in Mr Baber's lesson and I liked Mr Baber. He made the lessons fun and brought the subject to life. When the lesson ended, no one wanted to leave his lab, and if it was lunch time, he'd stay with us and have a chat with us until either he was ready to eat or it was our allocated time to line up in the lunch hall (this I'd do before I was permanently excluded from lunch at school). Many years after I left Fairfield, the education sector introduced the role of Pastoral Care within schools, and it was of no surprise for me to hear that Mr Baber was Head of Pastoral Care at Fairfield Grammar School.

For as far back as I can remember, I had aspirations of becoming a lawyer, and this was inspired by the TV programmes I watched, namely *L.A Law* and *Rumpole of the Bailey*.

L.A Law was set in an American law firm, featuring high-powered lawyers who handled both criminal and civil cases, and *Rumpole of the Bailey* was a British Television series about an elderly London barrister who defended a variety of clients at the Central Criminal Court.

When I shared my aspirations with some of the teachers at school, they'd look at me blankly and say *"You?!"* and I knew they were thinking of my track record of fights, detentions and exclusions and thought there would be no chance.

I left school after taking my GCSE's, achieving a few C's along with E's, F's and some Ungraded results, but I remained determined in my hope of studying Law at University and began to research as to how this could be possible. I remember receiving guidance to apply to college to study the Applied Sciences, which were equivalent to the GCSE qualifications at that time, and would give me enough points to move on to study A Levels. This I achieved at South Bristol Technical College in Bedminster, along with achieving qualifications in A Level Law, Sociology and English.

But before I tell you how I got into University, I need to take a few steps back and tell you about an incident that almost saw me being permanently excluded from college.

On no particularly special day, I arrived at college focused and ready for another day of lessons and some entertainment from my friends and peers. Whilst sitting in the canteen at break time, I was told by one of my peers, that there was a girl (who will remain nameless) who had been bragging to my friends of how she could beat me up. At first, I was surprised that my friends hadn't told me about this and then, I laughed and told them I wasn't interested. Those around me heard my response and began to question whether I was scared. It was also known at the college who I was related to, and I was teased as being the one to let the 'Denton' name down. Not fazed by these comments, I went off to my lesson.

Naively, believing that the hype had calmed down and that everyone had moved on, I entered the canteen at lunch time, and it seemed to be unusually packed. My friends approached me and said, *"She's here and she's been bragging again about how she can beat you up"*.

Feeling the pressure, I didn't respond. I spotted the girl in question, and walked up to her and proceeded to say, *"So I hear you've been saying you can beat me up?"*

At this, she began to smile and then laugh. I heard those in the canteen gasping in sarcastic shock, saying, *"Oh no."*

And then it was not long before the fight erupted. I'm not sure as to the duration of the fight, but suddenly college staff raced into the canteen and immediately I and my friends ran out of the canteen, out of the college, across the green towards an approaching bus. On the bus, everyone was out of breath from running, yet silent, no one was saying a word, I just wanted to get home, and was relieved that this happened on the last day of term, ahead of a two-week holiday. But whilst on the bus, I began to think about whether a phone call had been made to my Foster Carers.

Arriving home, I remember saying, "Hello," to everyone and waiting around downstairs to hear any hints as to whether they'd received a phone call from college about what had taken place. No call had been made.

A few days before I was due to return to college, I was at home with my Grandmother, my Foster Mums' Mum and we both heard the doorbell. I answered the door to three people, two men and one woman, who were dressed normally. As I am greeted by them, I'm asked, *"Does Judith Denton live here?"*

I respond, *"Who wants to know?"*

At this, one of them takes a police badge out of their pocket and says, *"I'm PC..."* as soon as I saw the police badge, I immediately knew why they had come to find me.

The police officers let me know that they've come to take me to the police station for questioning and that I'm under arrest. They ask me if anyone else is at home and I let them know that my Grandmother is there and everyone else is out at work. I also explained to them that I'd need to go to my room to get my trainers and my coat before coming to the station with them. At this I'm accompanied through the house and to my room by the female police officer, whilst the other police officers waited at the front door. I also let my Grandmother know that when my Foster Mum came home for lunch, to let her know that I'd gone out and would be back soon. I say this because I remembered her warning of *"If you didn't stop this fighting, you're going to end up in deeper trouble and when that day comes, do not call me".*

At the Police Station, I let the Officers know that I am in Foster Care and gave them the name of my Social Worker, who they duly contacted. My Social Worker didn't come to the police station, instead she got in touch with my Foster Mum and let her know where I was and what had happened.

As I was sixteen years old, the police officers had to wait for an appropriate adult to be present before they could proceed with taking my Statement. Waiting in the police cells seemed like forever. They took the laces out of my trainers and gave me a cup of water. It was too silent and I broke down in tears. Now I'd been brought up to go to Church and believe in God and through my tears, I began to pray. I said, *"I'm sorry that I had another fight. I didn't really want to. I'm not sure if you're real, but if you are, I need your help. I can't have a criminal record and I can't go to prison because I want to study Law. So please can you help me out, Thank you".* This was my first real prayer.

My Foster Mum arrived at the police station with my biological Uncle [my Granddad's rother], and needless to say she was not best pleased. Her disappointment and anger were written all over her face and the police officers stepped aside as she gave me a good telling off.

I was questioned, fingerprinted and photographed. It was a frightening and horrible experience. I was charged with Actual Bodily Harm and given a date to appear in Court. If I was found guilty, I'd either be sentenced for a term of up to five years and or receive a fine (depending on the seriousness of the offence) or receive a fine and or a community order.

My Foster Dad was home from work when we arrived at the house and the atmosphere was awful. My Foster Mum, who was very much still angry and upset, said to *me "I have one son and I have never been inside a police station and you...."* She didn't finish the sentence, but I knew exactly what she wanted to say.

There was no mention of putting notice on the Placement and that I had to leave, but the atmosphere was tense in the house over the next few days. I felt remorseful and said I was sorry and as a family we talked through what had happened.

Before attending Court, I was told that my college wanted to hold their own internal hearing, in order to better understand what had happened and why, and then make a decision as to whether I was allowed to return.

Present at the hearing, was the girl, her Mum, the Police, the Principal of the College another college Personnel, my Social Worker, my Foster Mum and me.

This was the first time I had seen the girl since the fight and I wasn't sure how to feel about her and or the proceedings that were taking place.

The Principal made the formal introductions and began to ask questions in relation to the day in question. Before he could continue, the girl asked if she could speak. I noticed that her Mum gave her a side glance, which she seemed to ignore and continued. Intrigued, I listened and heard her say that she had contacted the police prior to the internal hearing, to let them know that she would like to drop the charges, as she was the cause of why the fight started. At this I blurted out *"Are you serious?"*, with my Foster Mum telling me to stop talking. I was in shock. Could this be the result of my prayer? I believe it was. The police confirmed that they had indeed received the call and that the charges were dropped and that I did not have to appear in Court. I was relieved.

The Principal instantly welcomed me back to college and let me know that if this scenario was to ever be repeated, with people goading me to fight, I was to immediately come to his office to let him know.

Before we left the room, I asked if all the adults would step outside, whilst I talked to the girl. She was happy with this and asked her Mum to leave the room also. On our own, we both said *"Sorry,"* and I thanked her for dropping the charges.

Chapter 3 – Foster Care, University and Law School

After college, I took a year out of education and decided that I wanted to work. My Foster Parents weren't totally pleased with this idea, as they thought I'd end up wanting to make money and spend money, off track from my aspirations to study Law and with no clear direction about what I would now achieve in life. Somehow, I was able to reassure them that I would eventually go to University, but right now I just needed a break from studying. Reluctantly, they came to accept my way of thinking.

Throughout this time, I found myself working in various jobs such as Cleaning, a Cashier in a Supermarket, and then on to working as a waitress in a Hotel Restaurant and Bar. And YES I enjoyed being able to make money and spend money on what I wanted, with the downside of having to chip in to pay the home telephone bill, as mobile phones were not yet on the market.

The novelty of this life style, soon began to wear off, through subtle hints and reminders from my Foster Parents, along with knowing that my brother was now at University. You see, when we lived with our parents, I always saw my brother doing his homework, which motivated me to do my homework. We attended the same Nursery, Infant and Junior schools and he seemed to be the one with glowing reports, with me being close behind. So, knowing that he was at University, gave me the push

I needed to continue with my academic journey, as in my heart I didn't want to be another negative statistic of how society preserved a child with a looked after background.

Getting into University was another challenge I had to face, because whilst I did have A Levels in Law, Sociology and English, these subjects did not give me enough points to go straight onto a Law Degree Course. I remember feeling disappointed as I heard this information, believing my chances of getting into University were slim and that I'd never achieve my aspiration of studying Law, until on the phone to the admissions department at the University of Derby, I had a light-bulb moment and asked *"I understand that I don't have enough points to get me straight on to the Law Degree Course, so can you tell me what course I can do that will then get me on to the Law Degree Course?"*

The answer I received was *"You can study the HND in Business Studies for one year and should you obtain a Pass or a Merit, you can then transfer on to study Law"*. Sold! I shared the good news with my Foster Parents and began to figure out my next move, the reality of living away from home.

I wasn't able to live on Campus, as I had applied through clearing and all the spaces on campus had already been taken. Instead, I was sent a list of private landlords in Derby, where I found a three-bed house and shared this with one other student.

I missed being at home and so would make the journey by train or coach from Derby to Bristol every weekend in my first year of being at Uni. I kept in regular contact with my brother, who was at University in Northampton and who would come and visit me from time to time, to make sure I was OK.

I have to be honest and say, that I partied hard in my first year, but managed to achieve the Merits needed to transfer on to study Law.

In my second year, I became more settled and integrated into University Life, working in the Students Union and becoming the President of the African–Caribbean Society, hosting events to unite students from both cultures (whilst remaining open to students from other cultures) to understand the African and Caribbean culture and heritage and basically PARTTTYYYYYY!

Life was going well, I was attending my lectures, handing in my assignments on time, until I found myself in a relationship. It didn't last, and I was devastated. The pain felt seemed to have a domino effect on my thought process, triggering memories of the circumstances that led to me being taken into Care, resurrecting the feelings of being abandoned, unwanted, rejected and unloved. I stopped attending my lectures, stayed at home and couldn't get out of bed, believing there was no hope for me, thinking *Who was I kidding, this kid in Care wanting to study Law and become a lawyer?*

I remember being visited by another student I had become friends with and letting her know that I had decided to drop out of Uni and return home. She was having none of it, and unknown to me, reported this to one of my lecturers. On no particular day, when I managed to drag myself out of bed to attend Uni, I heard my name being called out as I walked through a corridor and was summoned to have a meeting with one of my lecturers, Ms Tina Hart. As I sat in her office, I remember her letting me know that she had heard that I was leaving, that she didn't believe this was the right thing for me to do, and went on to encourage me to stay on with reassurance of support to catch up on any work that I had missed, and that her door was always open if I needed to talk.

I stayed on at University and graduated with a 2:2 Bachelor of Law Degree.

My Graduation was attended by my Foster Parents, my Auntie (my mum's sister) and my Brother. My brother came with me to be robed, and as I got dressed in the Gown and Cap, I burst into tears. Not really knowing what to do, my brother hugged me and asked *"Sis, why are you crying?"*

I replied *"I can't believe I actually did it!"*

Knowing exactly what I meant, he smiled and said *"Of course you did, you're my Sister and I'm proud of you".*

My next step was to move forward and study the Legal Practice Course in preparation for a career as a solicitor. I applied to a few Universities who offered the course, and took a shot at applying to one of the top Law Schools in the Country, this was The College of Law, now known as The University of Law. I got in and was based at The College of Law in the City of York.

Having become used to university life, I quickly became accustomed to life at Law School, not only with regards to the studies but I also became the Captain of our netball team, making it a mixed team. I had fun there, with aspirations of specializing in Music Law, but although I did pass my coursework, my overall grade depended on me passing my exams. This I failed to do.

Disappointed, I decided to take some time out, to contemplate resitting the exam, and with help from one of my cousins, I began working for McGrath and Co. Solicitors in Birmingham, within their Criminal Law Department.

At first working in this area, I was intrigued, then case after case, I realised that this area of law was not for me. I watched how certain cases where handled in the courtroom, and my heart went out to the youth that would enter the courtroom and be found 'guilty', and thought to myself, *But for the grace of God there go I.*

Care Leaver

If you are in Foster Care at the age of sixteen, you'll be
given a Plan to help you make the transition from Care into
independent life as a Care Leaver. At age eighteen, you become
a Care Leaver and your Local Authority must provide you with
some support, including a Personal Adviser and a Plan. At age
twenty-one, you can continue to get help and advice from your
Local Authority and a Personal Adviser until you are twenty-
five, if you want to.

Leaving Foster or Local Authority Care
www.gov.uk

Chapter 4 – Care Leaver
and Leaving Home

Returning home to Bristol from Birmingham, I realised that I missed my independent lifestyle and seriously thought about moving out and getting my own place; but I was now twenty-six years old and hadn't naturally transitioned out of Care at age eighteen, and didn't have a Social Worker to show me how.

You see, when I was presented with the opportunity to leave at age eighteen (I was in care in the 80s and the age had not yet increased to twenty-five), my Foster Parents and my Social Worker had a meeting, where my Foster Parents informed my Social Worker that I could stay with them for as long as I needed to. They completely understood that they would not receive any remuneration for my remaining with them, however that didn't deter them from allowing me to stay.

But now I felt it was time for me to go it alone, and I had to start thinking about where I was going to live, how I was going to leave? Who was going to help me? I'll also hasten to add, that I didn't have the conversation with my Foster Parents about wanting to leave as things were getting tense and I didn't want to upset the apple cart any further.

That being said, I followed through with my decision and spoke to someone I trusted and was advised to apply for Housing through Social Services. Without going into too much detail, this proved to be a complicated and lengthy process, but eventually I was given a one-bed roomed flat.

The week before I was to move, I sat down with my Foster Parents and explained that I was moving. There were mixed feelings about my leaving, as I had become part of the family, but it wasn't long before they accepted my decision and gave me their blessing.

On the day of the move, I enlisted the help of a few friends who helped me move in to my first new home. So, there I was, new place, new start, new responsibility! Yay? Not quite....

I had no job, no furniture, just me and my personal belongings and had to quickly think about my next plan of action. My rent was being paid through Housing Benefit and I was signing on, but the Job Seeker's Allowance wasn't enough for me to live on, pay my bills and make my new place look pleasant and feel like home.

Finding a job was also a challenge as I needed to make sure that what I earned covered my outgoings, but the reality of stepping into the world of work and living on my own, came with a quick lesson. I saw that the Income Tax and National Insurance deducted from the monthly salary I had hoped for, made me short of money and worried about whether I could go on living in my flat.

Somewhat burying my head in the sand, I moved my attention to acquiring furniture for my new home. I purchased some of the items by way of a Credit Agreement and some items were bought by way of Loans. I created a beautiful, liveable and functional home, but constantly worried about my financial state, as I now had to look for new employment to increase my income, to make sure I was able to make the monthly payments on the Agreement and the Loans, pay my rent (as I was no longer entitled to Housing Benefit), pay my bills, eat and live.

On one occasion, I can remember not having enough money to place in the electric meter and bursting into tears as I sat in darkness, stressed out thinking about what I could do. An out of the blue but 'on time' phone call from my Biological Mum, which instantly relieved my anguish. She had called to see how I was getting on, and on hearing my distress, transferred enough money into my account to pay for the electric and food. For this I was forever thankful, as although moving back to live with my Foster Parents was possible, it was not my preferred option, as I was determined to make this new life work for me. I was determined to survive.

Chapter 5 – Care Leaver, My Mental Health and Therapy

Having found a job that paid me enough to take care of all my financial commitments, I went on to design a project to start working with Teenagers in my local community. I had an idea to help keep the youth of the streets and out of trouble, engaging them in the creative arts of Music and Dance. At first the workshops took place in my home, but as we began to grow, we moved to a larger venue that was made available, at no cost. We also went on to put on events for youth to showcase their talents to their families and the wider community.

In conjunction with this, a few of my friends and I began planning and hosting events that took place in the City of Birmingham, showcasing various Gospel Music Artists and DJs. I was having a blast, so I thought, but something was missing and it wasn't long before I made the decision to move to live in the City of Birmingham in search of love and happiness. I secured a flat and went back to working with McGrath and Co. Solicitors on a full-time basis, but as a Legal Aid Clerk, and still I had not made up my mind as to whether I would resit my Legal Practice Course exams.

I can't exactly remember the day or the time of when this happened but on no particular evening, it was late, I got ready for bed but felt an unusual heaviness in me, around me and on me. I thought that if I fell asleep, I wouldn't wake up and that would be my end. So, throughout the night, I fought to stay awake, panicking as it felt as if the heaviness was trying to take over my body and was winning.

It got to the early hours of the morning and I was exhausted. I felt angry and at the same time a deep sense of sadness. I got up and began to put my belongings in black bags and then into the bin. I did this with my certificates from School, College and University, my clothes and anything else I could get my hands on. This made me more tired and weary and I tried my best to stay awake but then I thought *You might as well give in, this is it, the end.*

With that in mind, I got changed and made a phone call to a relative to say, *"Goodbye".* I made the phone call to my Biological Mum. I could hardly talk and could just about keep my eyes open. I remember telling her how I felt and saying *"Goodbye"* and then hearing her suddenly screaming down the phone. At this I ended the call and sat in my flat in silence, waiting, just waiting......

Not long after, there was a knock at my front door. It was a close friend of my family. I now know my Mum had called him and told him to come and get me. I remember he came in and sat and watched my movements whilst giving my Mum a running commentary on the phone. I don't remember saying much to him, just answering his questions as best I could.

He then said to me *"Judith you're going to be all right. You're coming with me to my parents' house".*

The next thing I remember, we were at his parents' house and my mental health began to rapidly deteriorate. In my mind I began to travel back in time and ask for my Grandfather. In reality he was deceased, but in my mind, he was alive, I wanted to see him and he wanted to see me. I had lost all sense of who I was. When I was asked my name, a phone call had to be made to my home for me to hear my own answering machine message in an attempt for me to connect to the voice I was hearing.

A Doctor was called and on examination I was prescribed medication in the form of tablets, which I placed in my mouth and hid it under my tongue to be flushed down the toilet, as I thought they were trying to kill me. I heard voices telling me to jump out of the window as no one would care. At the point of hearing the voice, I saw that the window was open with the curtain blowing in the wind, but when I screamed *"NO!"* I looked up to find that the window was shut. Things got worse and I was admitted into hospital and placed on a drip as I had not eaten or had anything to drink for some time.

I closed my eyes, too tired to keep them open, I opened my eyes and family members were in the room. I closed my eyes, too tired to keep them open, I opened my eyes and there I am running away with blood coming out of my hand at the place where they had placed the drip. I closed my eyes, too tired to keep them open, I opened my eyes and see myself being restrained [being protected] by security. I closed my eyes, too tired to keep them open, I opened my eyes to see someone coming towards me offering me medication. I refused! I closed my eyes, too tired to keep them open, I opened my eyes and saw myself being placed into an ambulance. I closed my eyes, too tired to keep them open, I opened my eyes and saw myself in a room. It's empty, just me warmly wrapped up in a bed. I closed my eyes, too tired to keep them open, I opened my eyes and saw the room filled with members of my family, talking and waiting. I say *"Hello"* and make a comment. Relieved, I hear them say *"She's back!".*

Two weeks after being hospitalised under the Mental Health Act, the time came for me to leave. In my final assessment, I watched as the doctor kept looking at his notes and then looking at me. He seemed puzzled and then asked, *"Judith, do you know how you came to be in here?"*

I answered *"No, when can I go?"*

He went on to say, *"I can't seem to explain your recovery in comparison to the state you were in when you were admitted [pause] and we have not medicated you"*.

Unsure of how to answer, I simply said *"So, does that mean I can go home now?"*

He replied *"Yes, but I have booked an appointment for you at your local GP to be assessed as an outpatient in two weeks".*

On the outside, it was horrible. I can only describe it as feeling everything that moved in the atmosphere. I was scared. I also thought the 'Rapture' (the end of the world and all Christians had gone to live with Jesus in Heaven) had taken place and I had been left behind to await the Second Coming.

Emotionally, I felt a lot of pain, could not stop crying and some days could not even speak. I couldn't go out alone and couldn't even look after myself. It felt like a really dark time. I had visitors, phone calls, prayers being prayed for me, but I felt as if I was disconnected from it all, almost lifeless.

Then a family member, recommended that I should go to Counselling. This process, coupled with my faith in God, saved my life!

I engaged wholeheartedly because not only did I want to be well but I also wanted to know what had happened to me. Connecting the dots over a twelve-month period of weekly Talking Therapy sessions, I learnt that I had carried the painful feelings of rejection, hurt, anger and thoughts of being unloved from the age of nine [the time of being place in Care] into my late twenties. During that period of time, I had masked those thoughts and feelings by subconsciously acting as if I was OK, and I wanted to believe I was OK and that what I had been through was absolutely normal. Sadly, because I had ignored these thoughts and feelings, they had begun to snowball and enlarge with every disappointment that felt like the rejection and hurt I had felt in my childhood, but I was focused on surviving, and had not been taught to talk about how I deeply felt. Unaware of the signs, my emotions suddenly began to shut down under this emotional stress and heaviness, as I could take no more and had become severely depressed.

Through Talking Therapy, I had to break the silence, face the truth and unpack every emotion and then lay them all to rest. I had to remember how I felt about him, how I felt about her, how I felt about them and how I felt about ME! I also had to forgive him, forgive her, forgive them and forgive ME!

Here I can also share, that as part of my recovery, I travelled to the USA and to Germany to talk with my parents about how I felt about being placed in Care. Understandably, it was hard for them to hear, but we managed to get through this difficult conversation with forgiveness and hope of rebuilding our relationships from that point onwards.

I prayed with each and every step taken, and I believe God protected and guided me through this painful yet, life giving and life changing process, which I can only describe as me having to learn how to live and thrive and not survive, learn how to take some time-out to 'breath' and learn how to move forward and look after my mental health and emotional well-being. Now I also describe this process as being able to see myself, my life and my way ahead clearly, as it felt as if I had been wearing a dirty pair of sunglasses that had tainted my view of my life and my world.

Now I must say, that not everyone understood what I was going through and at one point I felt embarrassed and ashamed of what I had experienced because of the stigma that can be attached with being hospitalised in this manner, but that being said, I am forever thankful and grateful for those who walked with me through the whole process and continue to walk with me to this day.

Strange, some might think to say, but I am also thankful for what I have experienced and come through, as I now know that holding on to deep and painful experiences and trying to act as if everything is OK is NOT the key to living a genuinely happy, healthy, meaningful and purposeful life.

So, what do I do now to maintain my emotional health and well-being?

1. Acknowledge the negative emotions that I feel in a situation.
2. Try to understand what has caused me to feel this way.
3. Journal about these feelings and thoughts as seeing this on paper helps me to see the situation in context.
4. Pray, talking to God about how I am feeling asking to be shown anything else about why I am feeling this way and what I need to do to no longer feel this way.
5. Take action! I may have to talk to someone to resolve a matter, forgive someone, forgive myself or change my location
6. Talk the matter through with my Therapist

I also:

✓ Have a 'Positive Thoughts and Thankful' Journal
✓ Go for regular walks
✓ Listen to positive and uplifting music
✓ Sing and song-write
✓ For work related purposes, engage in Therapeutic Supervision sessions with a Clinical Psychologist
✓ Try to eat and drink healthily
✓ Go to the Gym and the Spa
✓ Enjoy road trips
✓ Surround myself with positive people
✓ Try to get eight-hours sleep each night
✓ Try to maintain a 'balanced' lifestyle
✓ Watch a good film

Now there's more that could be added to the list, but I think you get the gist!

Chapter 6 – Care Leaver and My Career

In 2002, I moved to London, ready for a fresh start, but unsure of what to do. Remember, I had studied Law, attained a Law Degree, attended Law School and was still considering whether I should resit my Legal Practice Course exam, to restart my journey towards living in my so-called 'dream job' within the Legal Industry. However, deep down inside I could sense that this route was no longer for me.

Having experienced the crisis, detailed in Chapter 5, I was now divinely gifted with Mentors, who challenged me to take my time to carefully consider my next steps. Trusting their insight, following their advice, coupled with my faith in God, I had a gut feeling that I would arrive at the right opportunity at the right time.

In conversation with a relative, the suggestion was made for me to hand out my CV to the high street banks in South London. I didn't know much about the Banking Industry, and thought to myself, *Ok, if I am to work in a bank I'll be happy with just helping people pay their money in and make withdrawals and take it from there*, and so I did as suggested. It wasn't long before I received a call from the Manager at Britannia Building Society (now known as the Co-operative Bank) inviting me to come in for an initial chat. I went along, it went well and then I was asked if I'd be happy to return for the formal Assessment and job Interview. I'll be honest enough to say, at this stage I didn't even ask any questions about the job description of the role I was to be interviewed for, as in my mind, with no banking or financial industry experience, I thought if I got any job, I would be working on the Counter.

The day of the Assessment and Interview arrived, and it was then that I was informed that the roles available where for a Mortgage Advisor and a Cashier. No guesses as to which one I was banking on! However, with seven other candidates in the room and all with relevant backgrounds in the Financial Industry, I had resigned myself to the thought that I wouldn't be successful for the Cashier Role, but did my best to present myself well.

Three days after the interview, I received a call informing me that I had been successful and they wanted to offer me the Mortgage Adviser Role! Needless to say, I was shocked! I think the person informing me of the job offer, could sense I was in a state of shock, and she went on to explain that I was offered this role because not only had I done well overall, but they saw that I have a natural ability to build rapport and cause people to feel at ease, which is an essential skill needed in this industry. She went on to explain, that they understood that I didn't have a Financial Industry background and were willing to train me up and pay for me to study for the relevant qualifications for the role, and that she had no doubt that I would do well as she had seen on my CV that I had the ability to study at a Professional Level.

I went on to spend twelve years in the Financial Industry working in a Building Society and then on to high street Banks, starting of as a Mortgage Advisor, then moving on through being headhunted or in search of a new challenge, in the roles of Financial Advisor to Senior Financial Advisor, attending meetings with Directors and Executives, to present the views of my colleagues, advocating for improvements to the working environment and presenting solutions as to 'how', as their 'Workplace Champion'. There was good pay, company cars and the perks of the job BUT... I began to question and think that *There must be more to life than this.*

Don't get me wrong, I enjoyed being in the Financial Industry and learnt a lot from being in a Corporate and Professional environment, but my zeal for the job and the industry was slowing beginning to disappear. I had grown in the industry and in every role I acquired new skills and did my job to the best of my ability, but didn't see myself going any further. Each day felt the same and I was no longer enjoying being there.

Cue my Mentors!

I remember having conversations with them about what I had been thinking and feeling. They understood, but were sure to remind me that I couldn't step out of a job into nothing as I had financial commitments, not forgetting the debt I had accumulated as detailed in Chapter 4, and so they, once again, encouraged me to think carefully about what I would do. It was here and whilst still employed, that I felt the need to design a Financial Education Programme for Teenagers, as I began to see that I had gained valuable insight and knowledge into managing money, something that I believe I would have benefitted from had I been taught this at an early age. I let people know that I had created this Programme and was asked to deliver it to certain youth groups. This I thoroughly enjoyed and the groups engaged well. From being a Programme that was delivered via a Workshop and PowerPoint presentation, I redesigned it to be a Financial Education Game for Teenagers, to help bring to life how to handle money in a fun and more interactive way. I was also asked to deliver financial education workshops for Adults, teaching them the basic steps of budgeting and debt management, and was doing all of this whilst still working full time in the Financial Industry.

Here, I was enjoying being able to deliver my Programme, and would use the quiet times during my day at work to continue to research and develop the Programme through the skills and knowledge gained at work, and I saw this as a win-win. I also got involved with the Corporate Social Responsibility Programmes established by my employers and found myself volunteering in schools, when the opportunity presented itself. But the more I worked on and delivered my Financial Education Programme, the more I didn't want to be in my office at work giving Financial Advice.

I think my Manager sensed that I had lost my passion and I remember him saying to me during an impromptu visit, *"Judith, if there's one thing I've learnt in life, is to know when to quit"*. I took note of these words and went on annual leave for a few weeks. Returning to work was a real struggle, but I still didn't feel that it was time to hand in my resignation.

A few months later, the effects of the Financial Credit Crunch began to have an impact on the UK Financial Industry, with my peers in other Banks being made redundant. I recall attending a meeting with my Team where my Manager tried to reassure us that we were not to panic as our jobs were safe. I must say that the meeting unsettled me as I instinctively felt that our Bank would be next to let staff go. Needless to say, what I felt happened within the space of a few weeks and we were given the following options:

1. Take redundancy
2. Reapply for our jobs and take additional professional studies to comply with the new industry regulations or
3. Apply for an alternative role within the Bank.

This I knew was my way out! Whilst the Bank worked out the finer details of the redundancy, I decided to go along with the process and reapply for my job, in the hope that my application would not be successful. Thankfully, it wasn't and I proceeded to inform our HR Department that I wouldn't be applying for an alternative role, and was now ready to take the redundancy offered. I was nervous, I had all these ideas but was not sure of what to do next... but help was on the way.

Chapter 7 – Care Leaver and becoming a Social Entrepreneur

Stepping out of one's comfort zone is never easy. It IS the process of stepping into the unknown, something you've never done before. I remember talking to a close friend of mine, who used the phrase, 'It's time to feel comfortably uncomfortable' and I knew exactly what was meant. Here I was, being made redundant, which was uncomfortable in every sense of the word BUT at the same time, deep down in my gut, I felt at peace, comfortable with what was about to happen, somehow knowing that I would be all right.

Within the redundancy package, my employer gave me the option of being supported through a 'Working Transitions Outplacement Support Programme', a Careers programme delivered by experienced personal Career Consultants. There I'd be able to attend workshops and have a number of 1:1s to help me figure out my next steps and move forward.

I talked this option through with my colleagues, who were in the same position and also with my Manager, but to my surprise, they didn't have a positive word to say about what was being offered. However, I felt that despite what they had shared, I needed to at least see where this road would take me as I had nothing to lose.

Upon attending my first workshop and first 1:1, I was pleasantly content with my decision to accept this offer. The

Careers Consultant named Dorothy, who liked being called Dot, was indeed the right person who I needed to meet and be supported by at this stage in my life.

I remember the first 1:1 session that I had with Dot, where she asked me to share with her my plans. I was hesitant at first, as this would be the first time, I would be sharing my dreams of entering into the entrepreneurial world and the reasons for this, with someone I did not know.

I shared with Dot what I had learnt whilst working in the Financial Industry and that I had designed a Financial Education Programme which I wanted to build on in readiness to deliver it in Secondary Schools across the country and to Adults.

Dot understood me, our rapport was instant and she challenged me to think and dream big, helping me to see that what I dreamt about was possible, and that I had gained transferable skills throughout employment and studies, that were going to help me in my next move, along with identifying that I had an innate drive and determination to achieve.

Dot also helped me to see that this journey would not in any way be easy, that there would be a lot of shaping and reshaping of ideas accompanied by research, research, research and actions, but if this was what I was passionate about, to go for it.

I also recall, Dot encouraging me to have a Plan A and a Plan B. Plan A included my entrepreneurial goals, and the timeline of each step. Here, Dot explained that the timelines were to be seen as a guide and that if I hadn't achieved a goal by that time, to not see it as a failure but rather see the positives in what I had achieved and to keep going. Plan B contained an option to look into being employed. This goal was important to my journey, as I needed to financially support myself until Plan A became a full-time reality. Dot explained that I would need to consider a job, that would give me the time and mental capacity that I needed to focus on Plan A, highlighting the reasons as to why this next job was not to be one with long hours, or filled with heavy responsibilities as then I would be too tired to even think clearly about achieving Plan A.

An important element to my new way forward, was the financial implications.

I had had a good job, with a good salary and had become a home owner, with attributing financial commitments, along with outstanding debts.

Dot and I saw that if I were to apply for a job to match my Financial Industry salary, then I would have similar responsibilities, long hours and no time for Plan A, but if I considered taking a job with a lower salary, I'd have the freedom to work towards my goals. This advice I took, but had to figure out which industry I would enter.

Now I remember having a dream, where I had a conversation with a friend about working in a school. I awoke from my sleep and contacted the friend from my dream to ask her for guidance on how to start working in a school, and was directed to contact a recruitment agency called Sugarman.

During my interview with the recruiter, I explained that I did not have the relevant qualifications required for working in a school, but proceeded to share details of my background of working with young people along with sharing my personal story. As he listened, I was met with these words *"Judith, I know exactly where to place you"*, going on to talk me through the role of a Learning Mentor needed in a Key Stage 3 and 4 Pupil Referral Unit.

Please note, I had never heard of this role and had never heard of a Pupil Referral Unit, but felt that this was another step in the right direction, and accepted the offer.

Working in this environment, I quickly learnt that Mainstream Schools would exclude Pupils sending them to the Unit, for disciplinary reasons. The exclusion was either for a Fixed Period, with a view for the Pupil to be reintegrated back into their Mainstream School or the exclusion was permanent for the Pupil to be integrated into an alternative Mainstream School willing to accept them, offer them a place and give them a chance. I also learnt, that some Pupils would not be reintegrated or integrated into Mainstream School, but would leave the Unit and go on to College or an Alternative Provision to move on to the next stage of Education or onto their chosen Vocational Studies. My role as a Learning Mentor was to support the Pupils to help them overcome any behavioural, social or emotional problems, affecting their learning and help them prepare for Mainstream School or their next steps.

Whilst there, I empathised with these Pupils and knew I could have ended up in a Unit, if they had been available when I had been excluded from school. I shared my story with those I was asked to mentor and encouraged them as best I could. I also asked the Maths Teacher if I could deliver my Financial Education Programme in some of the lessons, in the format of the Game, as I saw from the curriculum that this was indeed 'Functional Skills'. I was also given the opportunity to plan and host a 'Talent Show', involving the staff and Pupils, inviting Guests to inspire and empower the Pupils.

However, it wasn't long before I had a LIGHT-BULB MOMENT, when it came to my attention that some of the Pupils in the Unit were Children in Care. Naturally, I empathised with these Pupils on a deeper level, and on hearing my story, they could see and hear from someone who understood them and their journey. From being asked to attend Reviews and Meetings centred around the one Fostered, I was surprised at how the Social Care Children Services Department was totally different in contrast to when I was in Foster Care. As I mentored I gained in-depth insight into why these Pupils had been excluded from Mainstream School, understanding that their behaviour, emotional and social difficulties were rooted in their Care journey, having a detrimental impact on their ability to learn. Intrigued with this insight, I wanted to know if this was a wider issue and found information from the Department of Education, National Statistics relating to the 'Outcomes for Looked After Children'.

It was heart wrenching to read

"Children in Care are likely to have complex and challenging needs and must overcome extra challenges to achieve their potential.

They are also sometimes regarded as low achievers with low life chances on route to being a financial burden to the State, being a part of their own dysfunctional family, being homeless, having a lower take up of education, employment and training, poor mental and physical health outcomes in adulthood, have higher reoffending rates and placed at Her Majesty's Pleasure".

I also saw statistics highlighting that Children in Cares' attainment level of GCSE's were much lower in comparison to non-Looked after Children, and that the percentage of Care Leavers not in employment, education or training, was considerably higher than those young people of the same age.

Through this research, I went on to learn that the most common type of special education need for Looked after Children relates to their behaviour, emotional and social difficulties, with research also stating that Looked after Children and young people have consistently been found to have much higher rates of mental health difficulties than the general population.

I was saddened by what I had found, yet at the same time passionately hopeful of change as I reflected on my journey.

It was here that I knew my plans to develop my Financial Education Programme, had come to an end. It was here that I knew that I had to do something, find a solution to the problems identified by the Department of Education. It was here that I knew I had to help improve the outcomes and life chances of Children and Young People in Care and Care Leavers, and set about designing a Programme to make this a reality.

Through this developmental stage, I was able to implement parts of the Programme, which helped to see a Looked After Pupil integrate back into Mainstream School.

I then went on to research whether the Programme would be effective in a Primary School and a Mainstream School setting, with Pupils who were at risk of being excluded. In both cases, working closely with Looked After Pupils, in my role as a Behaviour Learning Mentor, I witnessed the gradual change in their focus and behaviour, which enabled them to remain in the Mainstream School environment.

During this time, I made the decision to film my Care Experienced story and upload it on to YouTube, along with writing a song entitled *Change is Possible*, which I refer to as the soundtrack to my story.

Whilst working in schools during the day, I went on to design and develop another Programme, which was delivered to a Looked After Children's Group in Barking and Dagenham once a week over a six-week period. Using my filmed documentary as a catalyst for discussion, I was surprised to see how well the group openly shared their story of how being in Care impacted on the views they have about themselves and how they were treated by the wider community. They also shared their hopes and aspirations as they were inspired with hope to see that achieving their dreams is indeed possible. At the end of the six weeks, I was pleasantly surprised to receive this letter.

Sadly, the Contract could not be renewed as a result of Local Authority budget cuts and it was here that my role as Behaviour

London Borough of
Barking & **Dagenham**

The Vibe
19 - 211 Becontree Ave,
Dagenham,
RM8 2UT.

Date: 19/12/13

Dear Miss Judith Denton,

I would like to thank you for the brilliant work that you have completed with the Looked after Children groups at the Vibe Youth Centre. I am amazed with the success of the project and how the young people engaged and interacted during the weeks working with you. The young people's feedback was very positive and they really enjoyed watching your videos and creating their books. I believe the book is a wonderful resource for the young people to look back on and reflect on their future paths that they want to take in life to succeed and reach their full potential. The young people was impacted on the sessions you delivered here at the Vibe, as they were able to relate to your past circumstances and were able to speak out, in a safe and secure environment. Some of the young people from Skittlz Children in Care council are now discussing some of the issues that were raised in your sessions ,so that they can work with the cooperate parents in Barking and Dagenham to overcome any barriers that Children in Care may have. Furthermore I have also noticed that the confidence in several young people have grown and have become more self motivated and inspired to achieve in and out of school. I have really enjoyed working with you and it's great to see passionate professionals supporting young people to achieve great things in their lives.

Yours sincerely

Naomi Ibe

Naomi Ibe
Senior Youth Worker – Participation

Phone
Email

INVESTOR IN PEOPLE

www.barking-dagenham.gov.uk   Most Improved Council 2008

41

Learning Mentor, also came to an end as the school I had been working in, felt that this role was no longer required, a decision impacted by budget cuts.

Reflecting on my time in the Pupil Referral Unit, Mainstream Schools and with the Looked After Children's Group, I realised that I had conducted 'on the job research' and was now armed with 'reasons as to why and how' I could help to make a difference in the lives of our Children and Young People in Care, but didn't know how to bring this to market.

Continuing to find jobs in the Youth and Social Care Sector, I took the time to look into how to prepare a Business Plan and steadily put this into action, along with subscribing to several Business Start Up mailing lists.

Receiving an email about the School for Social Entrepreneurs was another opportunity to point me in the right direction.

The email detailed that the School were open to receiving applications for their Lloyds TSB Social Entrepreneurs Start Up Programme in London. Initially intrigued and yet unsure as to whether this would be for me, the information explained that a Social Entrepreneur is a person who wants to use business skills to solve social problems, making a difference in the lives of a group of disadvantaged, vulnerable people and their community.

As I read, I understood that I passionately wanted to help solve the problems identified by the Department of Education and had a desire to improve the outcomes and life chances of our vulnerable, disadvantaged and marginalised Looked After Children and Young People, which would have an impact, not only on the individuals, but also on their community and naturally on Society and the State. I also identified with being a Social Entrepreneur and knew that I needed to acquire the relevant business skills to set about having social impact, and so sent in my application, waiting in hope for a response of an invitation to enter the second phase of applications.

Good news! I received another email, letting me know that I had successfully gained a place in the next phase and was invited to pitch my idea to a team of Executives. Note, I have never had to pitch or present in this manner, and took to searching on YouTube for guidance as to how, practicing as if my life depended on it.

The day arrived. As I sat in the colourful and welcoming waiting area, I was nervous. *What if they don't think my idea is good enough? What if others are better than mine? Can I even do this? What was I thinking? What if I forget what I'm supposed to say?'* And then I heard *"Judith, they're ready for you".*

I entered the room and saw six friendly faces smiling back me as I introduced myself, gathering my thoughts as I took my seat at the table. One by one the Executives introduced themselves and let me know to begin my pitch when I felt ready. I had three minutes.

Deep breath....

I began the pitch by introducing my story of being in Foster Care and the challenges I faced, I swiftly moved on to relate these challenges to the outcomes identified by the Department of Education and the problem this has on society and ultimately the State. I then moved on to detail the solution, born out of how, with the right support, I have been able to make it out of dysfunction into being a Professional, ready to reach back and make this change possible in the lives of Children and Young People coming through the Foster Care system.

I was then asked questions by the Group, about the Programme, before moving on to the 1:1 Interview Stage, the final stage of the process.

This may sound strange to say, but as I left the building, I felt confident and firmly believing in what I had to offer, as it was the first time, I had heard myself speak so passionately about something I created to people, Executives, I did not know. I also left the building with the view that if I did not gain a place on the course, that I would still go ahead and find away to make these plans work.

With just over 200 applicants, 40 successfully gained a place on the course and I was one of them!

Here I was awarded a £4,000 grant to help set up the Social Enterprise, I was assigned a Mentor from the School (one who had successfully completed the Programme), I was also assigned a Mentor from Lloyds Bank, and over a period of twelve months, I engaged in learning about business models, legal structures, managing finances, marketing, networking, measuring impact, along with leadership skills.

It was here that The Transformed You became my reality, established to provide **Intervention and Support Mentoring Programmes** designed specifically to transform the lives and raise the aspirations of Children in Care and Care Leavers who are identified as having behaviour, emotional and social difficulties hindering their success.

The vision is to support and develop within them a set of attitudes to build resilience, self-confidence, self-esteem, good social and communication skills and life skills, in order for them to achieve their aspirations and their full potential thus **improving their outcomes and life chances.**

Empowered through this course, I emailed most of the Local Authorities in London as a way of marketing and promoting the service and only received a response from Jane Hargreaves, the Director of Education within the London Borough of Barking and Dagenham. Jane, invited me in to meet with her to gain more information about what I had to offer, but to my surprise on entering her office, she introduced me to four Heads of Departments who worked with Children and Young People in Care in the Borough. Taking a seat at the table, I pitched the service, which led to me being commissioned by the Virtual School.

Working collaboratively with Social Care Children's Services Departments, Virtual Schools have been established by Local Authorities to promote the progress and educational attainment of children and young people who are or who have been in Care, so that they achieve educational outcomes comparable to their peers.

From here, The Transformed You continue to be commissioned by the London Borough of Barking and Dagenham, along with the London Boroughs of Tower Hamlets and Islington, working closely with the Virtual Schools, Children's Services Departments and the Education Provisions.

The Intervention and Support Mentoring Programmes are long term and delivered on a 1:1 basis, by an Intervention and Support Mentor guiding the Children in Care and Care Leavers through the following **4 Steps**:

1. **Identify** the root causes of their emotional, behaviour and social difficulties.
2. **Learn** how to overcome those internal and external challenges.
3. **Rebuild** their lives through being equipped and empowered with life skills needed to develop and grow with confidence.
4. To **Achieve** their aspirations and full potential improving their outcomes and life chances.

Our **Mentors** are role models who will share their experiences and life skills to guide the Children in Care and Care Leavers through the **4 Steps** and towards achieving emotional well-being and success.

Our Mentors are also:

- ✓ **Advocates** who elevate the 'voice' of the Child in Care and Care Leaver at meetings with Social Care and Professionals along with empowering them to understand their legal entitlements
- ✓ **Advisers** who use their expertise to support the Care Leavers towards achieving their **'Pathway Plan'**
- ✓ and a **Coach** who supports the Child in Care and Care Leaver towards achieving their specific goals.

The Transformed You also offer Group Mentoring Programmes, along with providing Training Courses to inform, empower and provide practical strategies, from a Care Experienced viewpoint, for Foster Carers, Social Workers, Teachers and School Staff, on how to support the one being Fostered.

For more information about The Transformed You, feel free to visit www.thetransformedyou.co.uk.

I've now gone on to being a Keynote Speaker at Social Care Conferences sharing my experience of the UK Foster Care System, along with providing insight and solutions, to inspire and empower the audience; and I'm also a member of the London Borough of Barking and Dagenham's Fostering Panel, positioned to help make sure our Children and Young People in Care get the best of Care.

And I encourage you to see and believe that through the details of my journey 'Change Is Possible' for you too!

Messages

To Inspire, To Encourage, To Enlighten, To Empower,
To Bring Hope and Call To Action.

Judith A.M Denton

A Message to Children and Young People in Care and Care Leavers

Whatever the reason, the reality is, you are now in Foster Care, separated from your family. You may or may not understand how you got there, and some of you may not even want to believe and accept the true facts about how you got there, and some of you may be glad that you are in Care but still have a longing to be back with your family, be that on a permanent basis or visit from time to time.

Now this separation can be seen as a distressing event, that has a traumatic impact on what you think about yourself, your family, your Foster Carers, your friends and others around you. It can also impact on how you express yourself, reacting or responding to situations that remind you of this separation. It can also impact on how you develop and move forward in life.

The effects of this separation can also cause you to look at your life, compare it to what you consider to be the 'normal loving relationships' of your peers who live with their families, and ask yourself, *'Who loves and cares about me?'*, with doubts that this love and care that you desire, could ever be possible, because it seems as though your parents who brought you into this world, aren't able to provide this for you, and so you search for that place of emotional safety, aiming to find someone you can trust, to accept and be there for ALL of you, on your good days and not so good days.

Continually feeling let down, unsure of how to navigate this new life, and fed up of being told what to do, you take to burying your head in the sand, aiming to escape from what seems to be the internal and external noise and pain, that reminds you that you are in Care and being treated 'differently' in comparison to your peers.

For some, you choose not to attend your Child in Care Reviews or your Personal Education Planning Meetings, but when you do attend you sit somewhat silently observing, listening to what is being discussed, sometimes wondering who are these people talking about you, but do not know you, and then excuse yourself in frustration of not being heard or misunderstood.

For others, your circle of friends aren't the best choice, but you try to fit in, to at least be accepted by them. However, these friendships tend to be short lived because of inner circle disagreements that first present themselves via Social Media and then when you are face-to-face.

For some, you check out of your world and run away and do so, finding yourself surrounded by a group of other young people, with whom you identify and see them as 'family', people who 'care', but then struggle with what you are being asked to do and desire to come home, but are unsure of where home is and as a result you start to sofa surf or become homeless.

For others, you make a conscious decision to escape through education, as the pages of every text book you read, help to suppress the pain of your reality.

For some, finding yourself in a relationship seemed to be the answer, until you noticed that this was indeed a replica of the dysfunction you were removed from, and void of the love you are looking for.

For others, the party lifestyle seemed appealing, with all the substances and alcohol that it has to offer to numb the emotional cycle of pain, but a look in the mirror has given you the revelation that this is not your way out.

For some, several Foster Care Placement moves, with your belongings being placed in either a 'black bin bag' or 'large see-through plastic bag', has left you feeling like a 'parcel being passed around' causing you to believe that 'no one really cares'.

For others, you have no faith in the system that is designed to Care for you, as meeting after meeting with your Social Worker, has left you wondering whether they are on your side and whether they have 'heard your request for Contact with your family'.

For some, separated from your siblings, living in different Foster Care Placements, has caused you to worry about the level of care they are receiving.

For others, being placed in Residential Care miles away from anyone or anything you can identify with, has left you feeling isolated and disconnected, brimming with anger at whoever made the decision for you to be there.

For some, you long for the day when you no longer feel 'controlled' by the System, but are unsure of how and when this will ever be possible.

So, where do we go from here?

As you have read from my story, understand that change is indeed possible for you too, but you have to WANT this change. *"Where do I start?"*, you ask, the answer is, with a small amount of self believe and say to yourself that *"I believe I can change and have a better life, with the help of the right people"* and then you have to find the courage to AGREE that you need the help (because the adults around you, and some of your 'real' friends, can see that you are in need of help) and make the move to do your best to ENGAGE with the help.

Now your first step towards any specific help you need, will be identified and actioned by either:

- ✓ Your Social Worker or Personal Adviser
- ✓ Your Foster Carer
- ✓ A member of staff at School, College or University
- ✓ Your Mentor

You can also be supported by any family and friends who are positive influences in your life and genuinely have your best interests at heart.

Taking these steps will not be easy, but I want you to understand that whilst this group of people identified are there to support you, know that you will connect with certain individuals more than with others. Based on that connection, that individual will stay in contact with you, advocate for you, may not always agree with you or tell you what you want to hear, but will be honest with you. Knowing this you must also reach out to them, especially when things seem unbearable or you feel at a loss. Don't suffer in silence, you are not meant to travel through life on your own.

Now, as you engage with this help to make the changes in your life, it is vitally important that your 'VOICE' is heard and UNDERSTOOD, as you use it to share your thoughts, feelings and wishes. I know that communicating in this way may feel uncomfortable, and you may not say the right thing in the right way and this may frustrate you, BUT don't panic, run away or stop using your voice, because learning how to communicate in this 'new' way takes time, it will get easier and you'll have the support from those who will understand your expression and help you make sense of what it is you are trying to convey and ensure that your needs are being met.

It's also important to note, that with each step you take towards positive change, hope for a brighter future will begin to emerge and become your reality with hard work and determination, along with causing you to become more self-aware and in tune with your abilities, which will rebuild your confidence and self-esteem, as you begin to see yourself accomplish what you thought you couldn't, gaining the drive and tangible 'know-how' of achieving your new found goals.

Your self-worth will also be rebuilt with every step, as you understand that you are indeed 'valued and are worthy of love and can give this love', as you first learn how to love, value and care for yourself.

Now if you've read this message and are a Care Leaver of any age, and can identify with what I have shared, then this way forward is for you too. It's not too late for change!

It's time for us all, to LIVE and THRIVE!

A Message to Foster Carers

Foster Carers, I am so thankful for you. You are the ones who open your hearts and your homes in order to provide us with a safe place, stability and love. You also plant positive seeds of hope in us, that help to begin the transformational process in us that will prepare us for our bright future.

Sadly, not everyone of us in Foster Care can testify of receiving such warmth and care. Some of us, whilst in Foster Care have experienced distressing times that seem to replicate the dysfunction we have been removed from. Some of us have felt that we are a 'job' to you, with payment seen as your primary focus and so are unable to build a positive attachment to you; and some of us have felt let down by you as you give up on us and send us on our way when we are going through our challenging and trying times.

With that being said, many Foster Carers will acknowledge that Foster caring is challenging BUT that it also rewarding as you begin to see the one you have chosen to care for, transform and blossom, positively making steps and strides forward, and that I do believe can be achieved with the help of the innate Super Powers of Foster Carers.

As I reflect on my journey through Foster Care, I've come to the conclusion that my Foster Carers possessed these 'Super Powers' that helped to save and transform my life, and I also see these 'Super Powers' as Foundational Pillars that will set the positive flow and tone of any Foster Carer and Fostered Child or Young Person relationship. The Super Powers are:

★ Unconditional Love
★ Acceptance and Understanding
★ Nurture and Patience
★ Stickability

I've written a Handbook called *The Foster Carers Super Powers* which details them at length, relating them to stories about my time with my Foster Carers. The Handbook is FREE and available for you to download at www.thetransformedyou. co.uk. Here I'll share with you a brief insight into the Super Powers, I believe you also possess.

Super Power #1 Unconditional Love

The first Super Power I experienced from my Foster Carers, was 'Unconditional Love'. They loved me through everything I put them through and I could see how much they loved and cared for each other, with no strings attached.

They also understood my 'Love Language', described as love actioned or expressed in a way that I understood and felt that I was truly loved.

Gary Chapman and Ross Campbell, wrote books about the 5 Love Languages for Children and Teenagers[1], provoking the reader to think about, 'How does the Child or Teenager know that they are loved by their parents or guardians?' The Love Languages are:

✓ **Words of affirmation**
✓ **Quality Time**
✓ **Acts of Service**
✓ **Gifts**
✓ **Physical Touch**

---

[1] The 5 Love Languages of Children, The 5 Love Languages of Teenagers.

Growing up with my Foster Carers, I knew they loved me <u>when</u> we would sit together and listen to Music and watch Movies **[Quality Time]**, <u>when</u> they'd encourage me to do better and give me guidance as to how **[Words of Affirmation]**, <u>when</u> we'd go out to eat or shop together **[Quality Time]**, <u>when</u> my Foster Mum would announce that the Ribena and Salad Cream that she had bought were mine and were not to be consumed by anyone else in the home, and when my Foster Dad surprised me with my first music stereo system **[Acts of Service and Gifts]**, and this Super Power of unconditional love was consistently felt, and has taught me to try my best to identify how the people close to me understand that I love them, unconditionally.

Super Power #2 Accept & Understand
The second Super Power I experienced from my Foster Carers, was their Power to accept and understand me.

Being placed in Foster Care, I felt unwanted and rejected, but with my Foster Carers I felt wanted and accepted as part of their family. I was included in every family event, went on family holidays, was introduced to their extended family and their close friends.

My Foster Carers also understood the pain, frustration and anger that would surface after I had any form of contact with my parents, be that on the phone or face to face; and they'd be on hand to provide words of comfort and reassurance that they were with me throughout this process.

This Super Power has taught me to make people around me feel warmly welcome, have an understanding of what they may be going through and try to help them as best I can.

Super Power #3 Nurture & Patience
The third Super Power I experienced from my Foster Carers, was their Power to nuture me with patience, and I saw this in how they would have to consistently remind me to do my

chores and show me how they should be done, until they saw that I had taken personal responsibility and developed the ability to get them done to the standard that they were pleased with and sometimes surprised with.

These lessons prepared me for life as a Care Leaver, and I've also adopted their methods of how to patiently nurture the Children and Young People in Care I now Mentor.

Super Power #4 Stickability

Another Super Power that impacted my life was the Power of Stickability. The Power to stick by me through not only the good times, but also through the not so good times.

In Chapter 2, I shared my story of how I was arrested and charged with Actual Bodily Harm for having a fight at College, and will say here that I thought this was the last straw for my Foster Carers as my behaviour often challenged them to their core.

Through this Super Power of Stickability, I saw my Foster Carers resilience and felt their passion and commitment to me, and experienced their efforts to plant and instil values in me, hoping that I would change the way I behaved and change the way I viewed myself, my family and my world. They'd often tell me that they wanted the best for me, and saw that I had the potential and a good future ahead of me, and I also saw their frustration when I'd make the wrong choices, but nevertheless, they stuck with me and I remained living in their home until I was twenty-six years old.

Now whilst my Foster Carers, had every good intention to do their best for me, with the aim of being at their best, in reality, there were times when they were temporarily deprived of their Super Powers by what I consider to be the following types of **Kryptonite:**

Kryptonite #1: Triggers and Emotional Blocks

Here I can share, that my Foster Mum and my Biological Mum knew each other before I was born, and through living with my Foster Mum it became apparent that they had unresolved issues between them. This would come to light, whenever I'd answer my Foster Mum in a rude or sarcastic way, triggering a memory of an argument she'd had with my Mum along with the details of how and when and who, with my Foster Mum concluding that I was like my Mum and didn't have any manners. This just made matters worse, as it was evident that my Foster Mum was experiencing an emotional block preventing her from being present in the moment to deal with the matter in hand.

Kryptonite #2: At a Loss, Unsure of what to do

Now when I was at school, my pattern of behaviour seemed to be on repeat mode, with my Foster Mum having to continuously attend school to meet with my Teachers. On reflection, I can sense that this challenged her more than my Foster Dad, who remained very calm despite the not so good reports received from school. In contrast, my Foster Mum would go on and on about what the Teachers had said, but would not see any immediate change in my behaviour. At a loss and unsure of what to do, she'd venture off to meet two of her friends, with my misdemeanors being the hot topic of conversation, returning home filled with hope and a new plan of action.

Kryptonite #3: Tired, Fatigued

Both my Foster Carers were employed in addition to looking after me and other members of the household. This was often tiring for them and so I'd either be sent to spend the Summer Holidays with my Auntie [my Mum's sister] in London, or we'd all go on holiday to Jamaica, were I'd also be able to spend a few weeks with my biological Granddad, Uncles and Cousins [for what could be seen as extended family Contact and Respite], before returning to the care of my Foster Carers, who were refreshed and ready for the next chapter of our lives.

Kryptonite #4: Own Personal Issues

Sadly, my Foster Mum was diagnosed as having Osteo – Arthritis. It was hard to see this strong and active woman slowly finding it hard to care for me, the household and ultimately herself. This frustrated her, as she fought to maintain her lifestyle and keep me in check. That being said, although my Foster Mum wasn't as mobile as she would have liked, she made sure I heard her voice throughout the home, as she'd call me to have regular chats with her to make sure I was maintaining the standards and values she had instilled in me.

Now, although these types of Kryptonite were evident in having a temporary impact on the Super Powers of my Foster Carers, it did not mean that they did not have the overall ability of being great Foster Carers.

With that in mind, I encourage to you to see that you too have the Power to <u>Unconditionally Love</u> the Child or Young Person, that isn't Biologically related to you, in a way that they feel and understand that expression of love. You have the Power to <u>Accept and Understand</u> them, the Power to <u>Patiently Nurture</u> them and the Power to <u>Stick By</u> them through the highs and lows of their journey through Care and possibly after Care.

Yes, there will be times when you will have your Kryptonite moments or days, but that does not mean that you do not have the ability to be great Foster Carers. In the 1980s my Foster Carers did not have access to a Supervising Social Worker, but you do and so during those depleting times, I encourage you to draw on their support and your Mockingbird Constellation [for those that are a part of one]. I also want to encourage you to actively consider engaging in Therapeutic Support with a Qualified Counsellor or Clinical Pyschologist, as this will help you to maintain your emotional well-being and mental health, that will be stirred, shaken and challenged, with some of you experiencing memories of a past that you would like to forget, and for others bringing to the surface a side of you you may not have seen before, all coming to light as you walk with the one you have chosen to Care for.

Finally, whether you Foster for a Short Term, Long Term, provide Short Break (Respite) Care, Parent and Child Placements, Emergency Overnight Care, Remand Placements, are Fostering to potentially Adopt a child, provide Specialist Fostering or Supported Lodgings or you are considering becoming a Foster Carer, I encourage you, to see that you the POWER to make a difference in the lives of the Child or Young Person, you have chosen to Care for or are about to Care for. The challenge is great, but the rewards are even greater and so hope for the best, believing that CHANGE IS POSSIBLE, not only in YOUR LIFE but also in the life of the one being Fostered.

A Message to Schools and Social Workers

Designated Teachers | Pastoral Staff | School Staff
Through The Transformed You, I have met and worked in a joined-up way with Designated Teachers and Pastoral Staff who, with limited resources, have taken the time to understand the Looked After Pupil and support them as best they can to see that they remain in the Mainstream School setting, and for this I sincerely applaud you. But whilst I have also seen this level of Support and Care transcend through certain Head Teachers and certain members of school staff, I have yet to see this encapsulate the entire school body.

I would also like to share that I have met Designated Teachers and Pastoral Staff who do not operate in the way described above. From attending meetings with them, because the Looked After Pupil has racked up a significant amount of 'behaviour points' to trigger a meeting, it is clearly apparent that they do not understand the Looked After Pupil in relation to what they have been through or are going through. This member of staff then focuses on the behaviour, seeking to manage the Pupil instead of supporting them, placing them on a Behaviour Report or subjecting them to a Fixed Term Internal exclusion within the School or External exclusion to an Alternative Provision or Pupil Referral Unit, which sometimes results in a permanent exclusion Off-Rolling the Looked After Pupil or a Managed Move.

Now I could quote statistics of educational outcomes comparing those in Care to those not in Care, but my first-hand experience provides me with this evidence, informing my insight that not all Schools are adequately set up to 'support' our Looked After Community.

With that being said, I do understand that school is a place for 'learning', however I do believe that 'learning' does not just equate to 'academic studies and achievements'. Learning also involves learning those 'life skills' of self-value that come through positive affirmations from school staff who understand us, see our potential and cheer us on with a belief that helps to form and shape our personality and character, along with helping us believe in ourselves, teaching us never to give up on ourselves, as they actively do not give up on us.

In contrast, when a Looked After Pupil enters a Pupil Referral Unit, the energy and motivation to never give up on themselves is converted into the energy of learning how to survive in this new environment, and sadly with getting caught up in the peaking order and knowing that they are falling behind in their Mainstream School Studies because of the level of work that is set, their hopes and confidence in achieving academically is diminished as they are then directly or indirectly positioned to think about and settle with a vocational course of study, when this may not be the best route for them in view of their untapped potential.

With this in mind, I do believe that the way forward for Schools, is to not focus and react to the behaviour, albeit understanding that the behaviour is unacceptable, but I ask that you aim to intentionally make it a priority to first understand the behaviour, looking into 'What is the root cause of this behaviour, emotional and social difficulty? and 'What is the Looked After Pupil trying to communicate?'. In the answers you may find that the Pupil is feeling anxious because of a pending Foster Care Placement move, you may find they have had contact with their Biological Family which has stirred up flashbacks of things they may have witnessed in their Care and has subsequently unsettled them, you may find that they are subject to bullying by their Peers but do not want to give names for fear of a backlash, you may find that they're unhappy with their Social Worker who has had to deliver some not so good news or you may find that they don't believe in their ability to catch up on the school curriculum and achieve, due to a late start to their school year or because of several school moves.

Please note, this is not an exhaustive list of root causes, but I hope this helps to provide you with an understanding of the complex challenges a Looked After Pupil has to overcome in order to achieve their aspirations.

From here, the next step would be to meet with the Social Worker, Virtual School Advisory Teacher and Foster Carer, to work in a joined-up way and find a solution to address this very specific need of the Looked After Pupil, and I will also add that it is imperative for the Pupil to be involved in the discussions, letting them know that whilst their behaviour is unacceptable, their 'voice' has been 'heard and understood', and that they will be supported to prevent a repeat of the behaviour exhibited, with a view to seeing them remain in the Mainstream School setting.

Now I understand that not all Schools have received training on how to understand and support a Looked After Pupil, and that not every School has the infrastructure and the required number of Staff readily available to imbed this training once received. In some school settings the onus is placed on one Designated Teacher based in a shared office, to not only support their Looked After Pupils, but also other Pupils not in Care, along with being on the Rota to Teach, making it impossible to address and meet any needs identified, before the matter comes to the attention of the Senior Leadership Team.

Here I believe the solution is for each school to have a 'Well-Being Hub', a safe, bright, sensory, welcoming and nurturing space for Looked After Pupils to make use of when they feel overwhelmed, are unsettled or are feeling low, impacting on their ability to focus and engage in their timetabled lessons.

The Hub will be run by the Designated Teacher and Pastoral Staff who are trained in understanding and supporting Looked After Pupils, helping them to overcome their expressed complex challenges, with a view to seeing them re-engage in the flow of the wider school environment and school day, reducing exclusions. Feel free to contact me, if your School requires Training in this area.

Where required, specific Interventions and Programmes will be sourced and delivered within the Hub, for the Looked After Pupil on a 1:1 or Group Basis.

The Team will also be responsible for making sure that ALL school staff in Teaching and Non-Teaching roles, attend quarterly training on how to support a Looked After Pupil and are up to date on any issues impacting the general Pupil population.

The Well Being Hub will then also serve to meet the needs of Pupils who are not in Care, aiding to create a more inclusive School environment.

Making use of this Hub will help to improve the outcomes of our Looked After Pupils, directly relating to a pathway that matches their capabilities, along with improving their life chances.

Social Workers

Reflecting on my Care Experienced journey, I can say that my Social Worker, Jeanne Gilraine, was very warm hearted and caring. She facilitated Contact between myself and my brother, turned up to every meeting at school to support me and my Foster Carer, would come to my defence and speak to my Foster Carer when I shared things that I wasn't happy about, and it was of no surprise to hear how she went over and above the call of duty to make sure my brother was well looked after and supported, in the midst of experiencing four Foster Care Placement moves.

Jeanne and I had a good relationship, and I found her to always be open to hearing and understanding my 'Voice' in order to actively make sure my needs were met.

Now working in a joined-up way with Social Workers through The Transformed You, I note that the 'Corporate Parent Role' of the Local Authority Social Care Department is filled with Social Workers doing their best to work within the 'Framework' expected of them, whilst at the same time attempting to be on the same page with the Virtual School, the School, the Independent Reviewing Officer, the Placements Team, the Supervising Social Worker and the Foster Carer, and doing so sometimes without hearing and understanding the 'Voiced' thoughts, feelings and wishes of the one in Care, to make sure they are included in the conversation that is centred around them, for their needs to actively be met.

I also note that Caseloads get in the way, which can cause delays in a Social Worker being able to respond to a request or call from the one being Cared for. The impact of this delay can lead to heightened anxiety of the Fostered Child or Young Person, causing them to make poor decisions as they attempt to take matters into their own hands and care for themselves. This delay can also leave the one in Care feeling despondent, disengaged and discouraged at decisions made for them but not with them, resulting in them having a negative view and unhealthy relationship with the System that was designed to 'Care' for them, as they believe that their Social Worker doesn't care about them and is not on their side.

As a Mentor for Looked After Mentees, I must say that I have witnessed good relationships between some Social Workers and the one Fostered, but in contrast I regularly hear these comments from some of my Mentees about their Social Worker and the Children's Services Department:

> *'My Social Worker never answers their phone!'*
> *'The System has messed up my life!'*
> *'My Social Worker never listens!'*
> *'I've had seven Social Workers and they've not done what I've asked for and I don't know why.'*
> *'I don't like my Social Worker.'*
> *'Everything takes so long!'*
> *'They'll only do something, when something bad happens.'*
> *'My Social Worker will have all the answers at my LAC Review, but I'm still waiting for an answer'.*
> *'I'm just a job to them!'*

On hearing these comments, I understand the perspective which is being expressed and readily attempt to bridge the gap between the Social Worker and the Fostered Mentee.

That being said, I understand that Social Workers must work within the confines of a 'Framework of Statutory Visits', but ask would it hurt to include that Social Workers also actively handle matters on an 'adhoc basis', based on the 'reasonable request Voiced' by the one in Care.

Now I also understand that Caseloads are currently an issue and that the number of children and young people being placed in Foster Care is on the increase, and so to give Social Workers this 'adhoc' flexibility, I believe that if each Local Authority strategically planned and actioned a 'heart capturing' recruitment drive, which included a care package to see that each employee did not experience emotional and physical 'burn out', along with devising a long-term retention plan, to see that Social Workers do not fall prey to the offer of working as 'agency Social Workers', this may help to increase the number of Social Workers which will in turn reduce the number of cases held by each Social Worker and provide the time and space to answer and action the 'reasonable request

Voiced'. This way forward, would not only see Social Workers able to build and maintain a healthy relationship with the Fostered Child or Young Person, but this way forward would also help the one Fostered to have a positive view of their 'Corporate Parent' and provide them with a level of consistency needed within the System, as they navigate their way through Care, whilst at the same time understanding that the System will one day not be there for them.

I do believe that this way forward will help to stabilise the mental and emotional health of those in Care, as being in positive consistent dialogue with their Social Worker about their life and future will help to reduce anxiety, fear and worry. It will also help to build their Social Skills, confidence and self-esteem through being a part of the decision-making process, empowering them to learn how to take control of their lives.

I also believe this way forward will help to enhance the joined-up working of Social Workers with Foster Carers and Schools, to deliver 'real time' solutions without delay, thus reducing Foster Care Placement breakdowns and subsequent Foster Care Placement moves or the need for Residential Care. It will also reduce exclusions from school along with less Children in Care having to spend time in a Pupil Referral Unit or Alternative Provision.

In short, this way forward will help to improve their outcomes and life chances.

A Message to our Prime Minister, UK Parliament
Secretary of State for Education Parliamentary Under Secretary of State for Children and Families Ofsted Chief Inspector and the Children's Commissioner for England

At the time of writing this book, Boris Johnson, you've been voted in by the Conservative Party to be their leader, and subsequently our Prime Minister, the leader of Her Majesty's Government, as a result of Theresa May stepping down. As Prime Minister you:

- are ultimately responsible for the policy and decisions of the government
- oversee the operation of the Civil Service and government agencies
- appoint members of the government
- are the principal government figure in the House of Commons.

Within the Prime Minister's Cabinet of Ministers, Gavin Williamson, you have been appointed as our Secretary of State for Education, and are responsible for the work of the Department of Education as it relates to:

- early years
- childrens' social care
- teachers' pay
- the school curriculum
- school improvement
- academies and free schools
- further education
- higher education
- apprenticeships and skills

Kemi Badenoch, you are our Parliamentary Under Secretary of State for Children and Families [also known as Children's Minister] within the Department of Education, whose responsibilities include:

- children's social care including child protection, Children in Care, adoption, care leavers, social work, local authority performance and family law
- special educational needs including high needs funding
- education policy in response to the race disparity audit
- safeguarding in schools
- disadvantaged pupils – including pupil premium and pupil premium plus
- school sport, healthy pupils and school food, including free school meals
- early years policy including inspection, regulation and literacy and numeracy
- childcare policy, inspection and regulation
- delivery of thirty hours free childcare offer
- social mobility including opportunity areas
- DfE contribution to cross-government work to tackle rough sleeping.

Amanda Spielman, you are our Ofsted Chief Inspector who is responsible for Ofsted's inspection and regulatory work. You are able to draw on the full range of Ofsted inspection findings to report on the quality of Education, Children's Services and

Skills, locally and nationally. You are also responsible to Parliament for the organisation, staffing and management of Ofsted, and for ensuring the efficient and effective use of resources.

Children's Commissioner for England Annie Longfield, you promote and protect the rights of children, especially the most vulnerable and stands up for their views and interests.

Now I make this connection as each role interlinks and should operate in a joined-up way and on the 'same page' basis, to govern and direct what is being delivered across our Country, as it relates to our Looked After Community.

I also make this connection as I do believe that irrespective of who is leading our Country or operating within these roles, it is vitally important that the Government understands that they are ultimately responsible for doing everything within their power to secure positive outcomes and positive life chances for the Children and Young People in Care and our Care Leavers, whom they now 'Parent'.

Making this connection, I also believe that regardless of the agenda of each Political Party aiming to drive forward the changes they believe the country need, there must be consistency in how the Government care for those in Care, without the newly elected Party and Leader somewhat disregarding the potentially workable way forward made by the exited Party and Leader.

In the light of this, it is saddening to see that over the years there have been countless reports highlighting the recurring issue of poor outcomes and poor life chances for those that enter the Care System.

May I cite findings from the Department of Education and the Rees Foundation as follows:

"[It is said that] Children in Care are likely to have complex and challenging needs and must overcome extra challenges to achieve their potential.

They are also sometimes regarded as low achievers with low life chances on route to being a financial burden to the state, being a part of their own dysfunctional family, being homeless, having a lower take up of education, employment and training, poor mental and physical health outcomes in adulthood, have higher reoffending rates and placed at Her Majesty's Pleasure.

Looked after children and young people have consistently been found to have much higher rates of mental health difficulties than the general population.

Their outcomes are continuing to be poor compared with their peers who have not been in Care, from education to home-lessness, prison populations to mental health, it is increasingly being understood that this is a failure of the System and not of the Children in Care or Care Leaver.

It has also been noted that there are those who have died since leaving Care aged 19, 20 and 21."

Please understand that I do acknowledge that there have been some noted steps taken by the Government and Department of Education towards changing the trajectory found in the above research, with information to be found in several archived online Reports. However, the information in these Reports, do not seem to effectively transcend or translate into what is needed by those who are in need and at the mercy of the System, before they become Care Leavers.

I do believe it is fair to say that we understand that the journey into Care and being in Care comes with a set of complex challenges that must be overcome, and so if we understand this from the outset, wouldn't it be wise for the Government and Department of Education to seek to implement a preventative process to change this narrative of negative outcomes as soon as the child or young person is placed in the System?

With that in mind, being a firm believer that 'Early Intervention' is the key and way forward to break this cycle, I would like to propose and advocate for this way forward.

To create consistency in how the Government set about caring for our Looked After Community, I propose that a Manifesto is created and passed as Legislation by the UK Parliament that must be implemented by ANY and EVERY elected Prime Minister and their Political Party, as it is understood that our Prime Minister, their Cabinet of Ministers along with their elected MPs all sit in and are accountable to our UK Parliament, who alone possess legislative supremacy and have power over all other political bodies in the UK.

The Manifesto will complement the Children's Act, detailing 'best practice and workable solutions' as to how to improve the outcomes and life chances of our vulnerable, disadvantaged and marginalised Children and Young People in Care and Care Leavers across our Country.

The Manifesto will be informed by Round Table Talks that include the National Bodies of Social Workers, Independent Reviewing Officers, Foster Carers, Supervising Social Workers, the Virtual School, Designated Teachers and Pastoral Care Teams, but will ultimately be guided and directed by the 'VOICE' of our Children and Young People in Care and Care Leavers and the 'VOICE' of our Care Experienced Adults, as we work together in a joined up way and in partnership with our Government, Department of Education, Ofsted and Children's Commissioner.

Also invited to take a seat at the Table will be leaders of Charities and Independent Organisations, that have been set up and established, using their means and resources to help make a difference in the lives of those in Care and Care Leavers. Along with outlining how to improve the outcomes and life chances our vulnerable, the Manifesto will ensure that the same level of preventative intervention and support along with any ongoing support, will be accessible to all Children and Young People in Care and Care Leavers, irrespective of their postcode.

With severe funding cuts to Local Authority Budgets, the Manifesto will set out how Social Care and Department of Education Funds can be ring fenced and accounted for within the Children's Services Department and Virtual School, to meet the costs needed to pay for the services required to Care for our Looked After Community, along with setting out how we can ringfence the costs for early preventative interventions, which when invested in the early stages of the life of the one entering Foster Care, has the potential to reduce the amount of money spent on Residential Care, and over the long term has the potential to put a stop to the need to spend significantly large amounts of money on placing our vulnerable, in a Secure Children's Home or within a Young Offenders Institution.

The Manifesto will also contain a List of external Agencies, who are seen and assessed as competent to provide the required objectives of early preventative interventions, improving the outcomes and life chances, empowering our looked after children to go on to live fruitful and healthy lives as Care Leavers. These Agencies will be regularly reviewed, to ensure delivery is on track.

With quarterly Round Table reviews, the Manifesto will be a 'Living Document' updated and edited to reflect the changing times and new solutions. The Manifesto will also evidence impact.

Passed as Legislation, the Manifesto, will eliminate the break in the flow of consistency and momentum of Governmental progress, that may have been made by the residing but soon to be exited Prime Minister and responsive Secretaries of State. Adopting this way forward will also make sure that the needs of the Looked After Community are not unnecessarily placed on the back burner whilst other matters, for whatever reason, are pushed to the top of the Political Party agenda.

"It takes a village to raise a child", is said to be an African Proverb which means that an entire community of people must interact with children for those children to experience and grow in a safe and healthy environment and that the villagers (the community of people) look out for the children.

The 'Villagers' in Scotland have noted that the outcomes for care experienced people have been poor for too long, and knowing that they can't keep doing the same thing over and over again and expect different results, have taken urgent steps towards tackling the issue, launching a 'root and branch' review of the 'Scottish Care System' supported by the 1,000 Voices campaign and Chaired by Fiona Duncan, calling on the First Minister of Scotland to listen to 1,000 care experienced people over the course of the next Parliament, and take action.

Fiona has stated *that "while the review will be complex and issues challenging, it will be the expertise of children and young people with lived experience of the system who will ensure a focus on what matters".*

As Chief Corporate Parent, the First Minister, Nicola Sturgeon, agrees that the route to long lasting change is through the voice of care experienced people.

It must also be noted that because the Scottish Parliament listened to care experienced young people, the Children and Young People Act was introduced with some really big changes made to care, and so it is known that when the care experienced voice is heard, the path to real change becomes clearer.

In the light of this very real, powerful and inclusive example, I reiterate that the Manifesto will ultimately be guided and directed by the 'VOICE' of our Children and Young People in

Care and Care Leavers along with the 'VOICE' of our Care Experienced Adults, who will be invited to take a seat at the Table, as catalysts of the change desperately needed in the UK Care System.

To conclude, like you and I, those in Care have one life, but the Government and Local Authorities, have a small window of opportunity, within this lifetime, to save and transform their lives and prepare them to function as positive citizens in the UK or wherever they choose to reside, and so I implore you to use this timeframe strategically and wisely and consider what I have shared, as the 'VOICE' of one who is Care Experienced and now working with our current generation of Care Experienced Children and Young People.

Thank You.

This is not 'The End'

As long as there are Children and Young People being placed in Foster Care, we must unite our efforts to passionately, purposefully and consistently work towards improving their outcomes and lives chances.

Judith A.M Denton

Epilogue

If anyone had told me whilst being in Care, that they saw that I had the potential to go on to become a Social Entrepreneur making a difference to and for the Children and Young People I identify with, I would have looked at them sideways, burst out laughing and said *"Yeah right, in your dreams"*.

You see as I look back on my journey through Care, it reveals that because of the trauma I had experienced, I viewed my life and my world through tainted glasses. I had low self-esteem, low self-confidence, low self-worth, didn't really know who I was, and didn't understand my capabilities and where they could take me. I also had to deal with coming to terms with life away from my biological family, was trying to figure out where I fit in and found this a challenge, internalising the growing emotional pain. I had also adopted a 'survival' mindset.

This translated through my behaviour, which made it hard for my teachers and those around me to discern and affirm what I would or could become, and so I travelled through the education system, as expected, yet aiming to prove my naysayers wrong, although unsure as to how.

As you've read, my life as I knew it, came crashing down as the emotional pain became too much for me to contain and hide, and with being discharged from hospital and on the road of my recovery, I came face to face with the reality that the foundations of my life needed to be reconstructed, so that I could be rebuilt, in order to live and thrive.

I began to grow in confidence, with every step taken and every opportunity presented, but there were times the 'old me' wanted to step in and stop me in my flow, with the temptation to allow the negative domino effect of emotions to take me right back to square one, filled with thoughts of *I can't do this*, but my faith coupled with support from my Mentors, strengthened me to remain on track with positive affirmations, fuelling my desire to achieve and live a full and balanced meaningful life.

In search of this meaningful life, I understood that I have a purposeful passion to see that vulnerable, disadvantaged and marginalised Children in Care and Care Leavers, are supported to get the best that this life has to offer.

As at[2] 31 March 2016, the Department of Education reported that there were 70,440 Looked After Children in England, a one per cent increase compared to 31 March 2015, and a five per cent increase compared to 2012. At 31 March 2018[3], there are 75,420 Looked After Children in England, a four per cent increase from 31 March 2017.

With this number continuing to rise, year after year Reports are consistently evidencing that the attainment levels of Looked After Children are lower than that of non-Looked After Children. The DFE's Report published in April 2019[4], stated that the most common primary type of special education need experienced by 55.5% of Looked After Children, is indeed social, emotional and mental health, having a detrimental impact on their outcomes and life chances, as noted in the National Audit Office Report stating, *"Children in Care are likely*

---

[2] **Department of Education/National Statistics:** 'Children looked after in England' (including adoption) year ending 31March 2016

[3] **Department of Education/National Statistics:** 'Children looked after in England' (including adoption) year ending 31March 2018

[4] **Department of Education:** Outcomes for children looked after by local authorities in England, 31 March 2018

to have complex and challenging needs and must overcome extra challenges to achieve their potential.

They are also sometimes regarded as low achievers with low life chances on route to being a financial burden to the State, being a part of their own dysfunctional family, being homeless, having a lower take up of education, employment and training, poor mental and physical health outcomes in adulthood, have higher reoffending rates and placed at Her Majesty's Pleasure".[5]

Now whilst steps have been taken to try and change this trajectory, I do believe that without the VOICE and insight of the Care Experienced, policies and procedures will be written by those who have not journeyed through the UK Care System and by those who fail to understand how to best support us.

It is therefore imperative that urgent action is taken to unite our arms, our voices, our skills, to sit at the table, with a united cause, led by the Care Experienced, to see our <u>Children and Young People in Care and Care Leavers as high achievers with high life chances on route to not being a financial burden to the state, being a part of their own functional family, not homeless, having a good and high take up of education, employment and training, good mental and physical health outcomes in adulthood, have no reoffending rates and not placed at Her Majesty's Pleasure</u>.

Change is Possible!

---

[5] **National Audit Office report:** 'Children In Care' – 25 November 2014

Ingram Content Group UK Ltd.
Milton Keynes UK
UKHW041012280323
419293UK00001B/4